BABY BLESSINGS

A Book for Reflections by Friends & Family on Baby's First Years (I.E. What a Cute Baby!)

Susan Branch

CEDCO PUBLISHING
SAN RAFAEL, CALIFORNIA

"EVERYBODY LOVES A BABY THAT'S WHY
I'M IN LOVE WITH YOU." *Pretty Baby*

Welcome to the World

KISS BABY'S OPEN HAND &
THEN ROLL IT CLOSED SO HE
CAN SAVE IT.

The love in your heart wasn't put there to stay,
love isn't love till it's given away.

NOTHING IS WORTH MORE THAN THIS DAY.
♥ Johann von Goethe

"Nobody has
ever measured,
not even poets,
how much the
heart can hold."
Zelda Fitzgerald

"*Every man's life is a fairy tale
written by God's fingers.*"
♥ Hans Christian Andersen

Sugar is Sweet and so are You ♥

Where there is great love, There are always miracles.

Willa Cather

You make my
HEART sing!

TENDER·MOMENTS

♪ "To Know, Know, Know You is
to Love, Love, Love You." ♪♫

Phil Spector

Home

" There's nothing half so
sweet in life as love's
young dream."
♥ Clement C. Moore

Too much of a good thing can be wonderful

" Imagination is more
important than knowledge."
♥ Albert Einstein

Then comes baby in the baby carriage. ♥

Home was never
Sweeter than now

_____

_____

_____

_____

_____

_____

_____

_____

_____

_____

_____

_____

_____

_____

_____

"Once in a young lifetime one should be allowed to have as much sweetness as one can possibly want & hold."

♡ Judith Olney

Seek not outside
yourself~
Heaven is within. ♥

what a smart baby!

LOVE IS LOVE'S REWARD. *John Dryden* ♥

THE MOST IMPORTANT WAY TO
SHOW LOVE IS WITH YOUR TIME.

There is surely a piece of divinity in us, something that was born before the elements & owes no homage to the sun. ♥ Sir Thomas Browne

♥ KISS A BABY

"You must always be awaggle with love."
D.H. Lawrence

The future belongs to those who believe in the beauty of their dreams. ♥
♥ Eleanor Roosevelt

"Fortunately for children, the uncertainties of the present always give way to the enchanted possibilities of the future."

— Gelsey Kirkland

♥ LOVE KNOWS NO BOUNDS

Love the moment,
& the energy
of that moment will spread
beyond all boundaries.
♥ Corita Kent

what a baby!

Baby Love

"To love what you do and feel that it matters —
how could anything be more fun?" ♥
Katharine Graham

Generosity, Compassion,

Courage, Discipline, Charm, Grace,

Goodness, Integrity,

Spirit, Joy, Enthusiasm,

Forgiveness & **LOVE**

Baby Magic

'Touch your fingers to your baby's
forehead, eyes, nose, mouth &
cheeks ~ tickle under the chin ♥.

GOOD TIMES
ARE
COMING

The heart speaks in many ways.

"All that I am or hope to be,
I owe to my angel mother."

Abraham Lincoln

There are only two lasting bequests we can hope to give our children. One of these is roots; the other, wings. ♡
Hodding Carter

Dreams

It's love, it's love
that makes
the world go 'round.
from a French song

FAMILY FACES ARE MAGIC
MIRRORS. LOOKING AT
PEOPLE WHO BELONG TO US
WE SEE THE PAST, PRESENT, &
FUTURE. ♥ *Gail Lumet Buckley*

Seek not outside
yourself ~
Heaven is within. ♥

TWINKLE, TWINKLE, LITTLE STAR...

It's the
little things
in life that
mean the Most. ♥

God bless thee when winds blow; Our home, & all we know.

FLORENCE BONE

"LET ME KISS IT
& MAKE IT WELL."

LOVE IS HEAVEN AND
HEAVEN IS LOVE. Sir Walter Scott

Here's to the little,
to the tiny,
to the small;
To the ones that aren't big,
And to those that aren't tall. ♡

soft, snuggly, and sweet

BUNDLE OF JOY

When this you see
Remember me ♥

You'll always be my Baby. ♥

And may you stay forever young!